AF689138

Financial Freedom

Financial Freedom

Matthew Petchinsky

1

Financial Freedom: Building Wealth in the Modern Age
By: Matthew Petchinsky

Introduction: A Strategic Approach to Achieving Financial Independence Through Smart Money Management

Financial freedom is not a myth—it is a deliberate and strategic pursuit that anyone can achieve with the right knowledge, discipline, and mindset. In today's fast-paced, unpredictable economy, mastering financial independence is more crucial than ever. Whether you are just starting your journey, buried under debt, or looking to optimize your wealth-building strategy, the key to success lies in smart money management. This book, *Financial Freedom: Building Wealth in the Modern Age*, serves as your comprehensive guide to achieving lasting financial independence by leveraging time-tested strategies and modern financial tools.

Understanding Financial Freedom

At its core, financial freedom means having the financial resources to live life on your terms without being constrained by a paycheck or the fear of unexpected expenses. It is about having the ability to make choices—whether that means retiring early, traveling the world, starting a passion-driven business, or simply securing your family's future. Achieving financial independence is not about getting rich overnight; it is about creating a sustainable, well-planned approach to earning, saving, investing, and spending wisely.

The Importance of a Strategic Approach

Too often, people equate financial success with earning a high income, but true wealth-building is not just about how much money you make—it's about how well you manage and grow what you earn. Many high-income earners struggle financially because they lack financial literacy and discipline. Without a structured approach to saving, investing, and budgeting, even a six-figure salary can lead to financial ruin.

This book is designed to help you adopt a strategic and systematic approach to financial management. By implementing proven wealth-building strategies, you will learn how to:

1. **Develop a Wealth Mindset** – Cultivate habits and beliefs that support long-term financial success.
2. **Master Budgeting and Expense Management** – Create a foolproof budgeting system that ensures you always live within your means.
3. **Build a Strong Emergency Fund** – Prepare for financial setbacks without disrupting your wealth-building plan.
4. **Eliminate Debt Efficiently** – Use smart debt repayment strategies to free yourself from high-interest liabilities.
5. **Maximize Your Income Streams** – Explore multiple income sources to reduce reliance on a single paycheck.
6. **Invest Wisely for the Future** – Learn how to grow your money through stocks, real estate, and other investment vehicles.
7. **Leverage Passive Income** – Build long-term wealth by creating income streams that generate money even while you sleep.
8. **Understand Tax Strategies** – Reduce your tax burden legally and maximize your earnings.
9. **Plan for Retirement Early** – Secure your financial future by preparing for retirement at every stage of life.
10. **Achieve True Financial Independence** – Reach a stage where work becomes optional, and your investments support your desired lifestyle.

Why Financial Independence is More Important Than Ever

We live in an age of economic uncertainty—rising inflation, job automation, unpredictable market fluctuations, and global events can all impact financial security. Unlike previous generations, who relied on pension plans and stable job markets, today's workers must take full control of their financial destiny. Without a proactive plan, financial security remains elusive.

Moreover, the modern financial landscape offers unprecedented opportunities. The rise of technology, digital assets, online businesses, and alternative investments have transformed the way people build wealth. Financial independence is no longer reserved for the elite; it is now achievable for anyone willing to apply smart money management principles and take decisive action.

Overcoming Common Financial Pitfalls

Many people struggle with financial instability due to poor money habits, lack of education, and a consumer-driven mindset. Society often promotes reckless spending, keeping people trapped in a cycle of living paycheck to paycheck. By understanding and addressing common financial pitfalls, you can break free from this cycle and build lasting wealth.

Some of the most common barriers to financial independence include:

- **Lack of Financial Education** – Many schools do not teach financial literacy, leaving individuals unprepared to manage money effectively.
- **Debt Overload** – Credit card debt, student loans, and other liabilities prevent people from growing their wealth.
- **Failure to Invest** – Keeping money in a savings account instead of investing results in lost opportunities for wealth accumulation.
- **Lifestyle Inflation** – As income increases, so do expenses, making it difficult to save and invest effectively.
- **Fear of Taking Financial Risks** – Avoiding investment opportunities due to fear or lack of knowledge can hinder financial growth.

This book will help you identify and eliminate these financial pitfalls, replacing them with sound strategies that lead to long-term stability and prosperity.

A Step-by-Step Blueprint for Wealth-Building

Throughout this book, you will find actionable steps, real-life case studies, and practical exercises designed to help you implement what you learn. Whether you are looking to escape the cycle of debt, increase your income, or retire early, this book provides a clear roadmap to financial independence.

By the time you reach the final chapter, you will have the tools, strategies, and confidence to take control of your financial future. Every wealth-building journey is unique, but the principles of financial freedom remain the same—discipline, education, and strategic planning.

Financial independence is not a distant dream; it is a realistic and attainable goal. The journey starts now.

Let's begin.

Chapter 1: The Foundations of Wealth: Understanding Financial Literacy

Wealth is not just about the amount of money in your bank account—it is about understanding how money works, making informed decisions, and using financial knowledge to build long-term stability. Financial literacy is the foundation of financial independence. Without it, even those who earn high incomes can find themselves drowning in debt, living paycheck to paycheck, or struggling to maintain a secure future.

In this chapter, we will break down the core principles of financial literacy, why it is essential for wealth-building, and how you can develop a strong financial foundation that supports lifelong prosperity.

1.1 What is Financial Literacy?

Financial literacy is the ability to understand and effectively apply various financial skills, including budgeting, investing, saving, debt management, and retirement planning. It involves knowing how money flows, how to make it work for you, and how to avoid financial pitfalls that keep people trapped in a cycle of struggle.

A financially literate person:

- Understands how to create and stick to a budget.
- Knows the basics of saving and investing.
- Avoids excessive debt and uses credit wisely.
- Prepares for financial emergencies.
- Plans for long-term financial goals, such as homeownership, education, and retirement.
- Recognizes and avoids financial scams and poor investments.

Unfortunately, financial literacy is not commonly taught in schools, and many people enter adulthood without a clear understanding of how to manage their finances. This lack of education often leads to debt, poor spending habits, and financial insecurity.

1.2 The Cost of Financial Illiteracy

Many people assume that financial struggles stem from a lack of income. However, studies show that even high-income earners can face financial ruin if they lack money management skills.

The consequences of financial illiteracy include:

- **Debt Accumulation:** Without knowledge of how interest rates and credit work, people often accumulate excessive debt through credit cards, payday loans, and student loans.
- **Poor Spending Habits:** A lack of budgeting skills leads to living paycheck to paycheck and struggling to afford essential needs.
- **No Emergency Fund:** Many people do not save for unexpected expenses, resulting in financial crises when medical bills, car repairs, or job losses arise.
- **Failure to Invest:** Without understanding investments, people either avoid them completely or make poor choices that do not maximize their wealth.
- **Lack of Retirement Planning:** Many individuals do not start saving for retirement early, leaving them financially vulnerable in their later years.

According to recent studies, nearly 60% of adults do not have enough savings to cover a $1,000 emergency expense. This lack of preparedness highlights why financial literacy is essential—it allows you to make informed decisions that lead to financial security.

1.3 The Core Pillars of Financial Literacy

Achieving financial independence requires mastering the key pillars of financial literacy. These core principles serve as the foundation for building wealth and ensuring long-term financial success.

1.3.1 Budgeting: The Blueprint for Financial Success

Budgeting is one of the most important financial skills you can develop. It helps you control your spending, track your income, and ensure that you are allocating money toward your priorities.

A strong budget should include:

- **Income Sources:** Your salary, side hustle earnings, rental income, and any other sources of revenue.
- **Fixed Expenses:** Rent/mortgage, insurance, utilities, car payments, and loan repayments.
- **Variable Expenses:** Groceries, entertainment, dining out, clothing, and discretionary spending.
- **Savings & Investments:** Contributions to emergency funds, retirement accounts, and other investment vehicles.

One of the most effective budgeting strategies is the **50/30/20 Rule**, which allocates:

- **50%** of income to needs (housing, bills, food).
- **30%** to wants (entertainment, travel, hobbies).
- **20%** to savings and debt repayment.

By tracking where your money goes, you can identify wasteful spending and redirect funds toward wealth-building activities.

1.3.2 Saving: The Key to Financial Security

Savings act as a safety net for financial emergencies and future goals. There are different types of savings that serve different purposes:

- **Emergency Fund:** Covers unexpected expenses like medical bills, car repairs, or job loss. Experts recommend having at least **3-6 months' worth of living expenses** saved.
- **Short-Term Savings:** Money set aside for upcoming expenses, such as vacations, home repairs, or large purchases.
- **Long-Term Savings:** Funds allocated for retirement, homeownership, or major financial goals.

An easy way to build savings is through **automated transfers**, which ensure that money is set aside before you have the chance to spend it.

1.3.3 Debt Management: Controlling Borrowed Money

Not all debt is bad, but mismanaging debt can prevent wealth accumulation. There are two types of debt:

- **Good Debt:** Debt that increases your wealth over time, such as mortgages, student loans (if they lead to higher earnings), and business loans.
- **Bad Debt:** High-interest debt that drains wealth, such as credit card balances, payday loans, and personal loans used for non-essential purchases.

Two popular strategies for debt repayment are:

- **The Snowball Method:** Paying off the smallest debts first to gain momentum.
- **The Avalanche Method:** Paying off the highest-interest debts first to minimize costs over time.

Eliminating high-interest debt as quickly as possible frees up money for savings and investments.

1.3.4 Investing: Growing Your Wealth

Investing allows you to grow your money and achieve financial independence faster. Key investment options include:

- **Stock Market:** Investing in individual stocks, index funds, or ETFs to build long-term wealth.
- **Real Estate:** Owning property that generates rental income and appreciates in value.
- **Retirement Accounts:** Contributing to accounts like 401(k)s, IRAs, and Roth IRAs to secure your future.
- **Business & Passive Income Streams:** Creating side businesses or passive income sources that generate wealth over time.

The earlier you start investing, the more you benefit from **compound interest**, which allows your investments to grow exponentially.

1.3.5 Retirement Planning: Securing Your Future

Many people delay retirement planning, assuming they have plenty of time. However, the earlier you start, the more financially secure you will be in your later years.

Retirement planning includes:

- **Employer-Sponsored Plans:** 401(k) accounts, often with employer-matching contributions.
- **Individual Retirement Accounts (IRAs):** Tax-advantaged investment accounts for long-term savings.
- **Passive Income Streams:** Rental properties, dividend stocks, and side businesses that generate income during retirement.

Setting retirement goals early ensures that you do not have to rely solely on Social Security or government assistance.

1.4 Developing a Financial Growth Mindset

Beyond understanding financial concepts, a wealth-building mindset is essential. This means:

- **Delaying Gratification:** Sacrificing short-term pleasure for long-term gain.
- **Continuous Learning:** Staying informed about financial trends, investment opportunities, and money management strategies.
- **Setting Clear Financial Goals:** Defining short-term, medium-term, and long-term goals and developing a plan to achieve them.
- **Surrounding Yourself with Financially Savvy People:** Learning from those who have successfully built wealth and avoiding negative financial influences.

By adopting a financial growth mindset, you position yourself to make smarter decisions that lead to long-term prosperity.

1.5 Conclusion: Laying the Foundation for Financial Independence

Financial literacy is the first step to achieving financial independence. By mastering budgeting, saving, debt management, investing, and retirement planning, you build a strong foundation for wealth accumulation. The key is not just earning money but making money work for you through smart financial habits and strategic decision-making.

As you move forward in this book, you will learn how to apply these principles in real-life scenarios, create a personalized financial plan, and take actionable steps toward lasting financial freedom.

The journey to wealth starts now. Let's build it together.

Chapter 2: Budgeting Like a Pro: Tracking Income and Expenses

Budgeting is the foundation of financial success. No matter how much money you earn, if you do not manage it effectively, financial freedom will remain out of reach. A well-structured budget allows you to take full control of your finances, ensuring that you know exactly where your money is going and how you can maximize your savings and investments.

In this chapter, we will explore the essential components of budgeting, how to track your income and expenses effectively, and proven strategies to build a sustainable financial plan that supports your long-term wealth-building goals.

2.1 The Importance of Budgeting

Many people assume that budgeting is restrictive, but in reality, it is empowering. A solid budget gives you a clear picture of your financial situation and helps you make informed decisions about spending, saving, and investing.

The Benefits of Budgeting:

- **Provides Financial Clarity:** Helps you understand your cash flow, where your money is going, and where adjustments can be made.
- **Prevents Overspending:** Ensures that you do not spend beyond your means, helping you avoid debt.
- **Helps Build Savings:** Allows you to prioritize saving for emergencies, investments, and future goals.
- **Eliminates Financial Stress:** Reduces anxiety by giving you a plan for covering expenses and reaching financial goals.
- **Accelerates Debt Payoff:** Helps you allocate extra money toward debt reduction, speeding up financial freedom.
- **Enables Financial Independence:** A strong budget aligns with long-term financial planning, allowing you to invest in opportunities that grow your wealth.

Regardless of your income level, proper budgeting is key to financial success. The difference between those who struggle financially and those who achieve wealth often comes down to how well they manage their money.

2.2 Understanding Your Income

Your budget starts with knowing exactly how much money you bring in. Income includes more than just your paycheck—it encompasses all sources of earnings.

Types of Income to Track:

1. **Primary Income:** Salary, wages, or self-employment earnings.
2. **Side Hustles:** Freelance work, gig economy jobs, or part-time earnings.
3. **Investment Income:** Dividends, interest, rental income, and stock market returns.
4. **Passive Income:** Royalties, affiliate marketing, digital products, and real estate income.
5. **Government Benefits:** Social Security, disability, unemployment benefits, or stimulus payments.

When budgeting, always use your **net income** (income after taxes and deductions) rather than gross income to get an accurate financial picture.

2.3 Tracking Expenses: Where Is Your Money Going?

One of the biggest financial pitfalls is not knowing where your money goes. Many people struggle to save because small, unnecessary expenses add up over time.

Categories of Expenses:

Expenses fall into three major categories:

1. **Fixed Expenses (Essentials):** Recurring costs that remain stable each month.
    - Rent/Mortgage
    - Car payment
    - Insurance (health, auto, home)
    - Loan payments
    - Internet and utilities
2. **Variable Expenses (Flexible but Necessary):** These fluctuate but are still required for daily living.
    - Groceries
    - Gas/Transportation
    - Phone bill
    - Health care expenses
    - Childcare
3. **Discretionary Spending (Wants vs. Needs):** Non-essential expenses that impact savings.
    - Entertainment (Netflix, movies, concerts)
    - Dining out
    - Shopping for clothes, gadgets, and hobbies
    - Travel and vacations
    - Subscription services (gym, magazines, online platforms)

To gain control over spending, you must **track every expense**—even small purchases like coffee or impulse buys.

2.4 Methods for Tracking Income and Expenses

There are several effective ways to track your income and expenses. Choose a method that works best for your lifestyle and financial habits.

1. The Traditional Notebook Method

Write down your income and every expense in a notebook. This is simple but requires dedication.

2. Spreadsheet Budgeting

Using Excel or Google Sheets allows you to automate calculations and track spending more efficiently. Categories and formulas help you see trends in your financial habits.

3. Budgeting Apps

Apps like **Mint, YNAB (You Need a Budget), PocketGuard, or EveryDollar** automatically track your spending by linking to your bank account. These apps categorize expenses and provide real-time insights.

4. The Envelope System

A cash-based method where you divide your spending into physical envelopes (e.g., groceries, dining, entertainment). Once an envelope is empty, you cannot spend more in that category.

5. Bank and Credit Card Statements

Reviewing bank statements regularly helps you spot trends, unnecessary spending, and subscription fees you may have forgotten about.

Regardless of the method you choose, the key is consistency. By tracking where your money is going, you gain full control of your financial life.

2.5 The Best Budgeting Strategies

Once you have tracked your income and expenses, it is time to create a structured budget that aligns with your financial goals.

1. The 50/30/20 Rule (Simple & Effective)

This method divides your income into three categories:

- **50% for Needs (Essentials):** Rent, bills, groceries, transportation.
- **30% for Wants:** Dining out, entertainment, hobbies, shopping.
- **20% for Savings & Debt Repayment:** Emergency fund, retirement, debt payoff, investments.

This approach is beginner-friendly and ensures balanced financial management.

2. The Zero-Based Budget (Every Dollar Has a Job)

With this method, you allocate every dollar of income toward specific expenses, savings, or debt payments. At the end of the month, your balance should be **zero** because every dollar is assigned a purpose.

3. The Pay Yourself First Method

Before paying bills or spending on expenses, **set aside savings and investments first.** Automate transfers to savings accounts so you are consistently growing your wealth.

4. The Cash Flow Budget (For Entrepreneurs & Freelancers)

This approach is ideal for people with irregular incomes. It prioritizes covering essential costs first, then allocating the remaining funds toward savings and variable expenses.

5. The Anti-Budget (For Minimalists)

Instead of tracking every category, you set aside a fixed amount for savings and essential expenses, and then freely spend the rest. This method works well for disciplined individuals.

Choosing the right budgeting method depends on your personality, income type, and financial goals. The most important part is to **stick with it consistently**.

2.6 Cutting Unnecessary Expenses & Boosting Savings

To free up more money for savings and investments, you need to minimize unnecessary expenses.

Tips for Reducing Expenses:

- **Eliminate Subscriptions You Don't Use:** Cancel unused memberships and streaming services.
- **Cook at Home:** Reduce dining out and meal prep instead.
- **Use Cash-Back Apps:** Leverage apps like Rakuten or Honey for discounts and cash-back rewards.
- **Negotiate Bills:** Call service providers to negotiate lower rates on internet, phone, or insurance.
- **Shop Smarter:** Buy in bulk, use coupons, and wait for sales.
- **Switch to Generic Brands:** Save money by avoiding brand-name products.

Every dollar saved can be redirected toward your financial goals.

2.7 Conclusion: Budgeting is the Key to Financial Independence

A well-structured budget is the roadmap to financial freedom. By **tracking your income and expenses, choosing a budgeting method that works for you, and cutting unnecessary costs,** you set yourself up for long-term wealth-building.

Remember, budgeting is not about restricting yourself—it is about **empowering yourself** to achieve financial security and independence.

The next step in your journey is learning **how to eliminate debt effectively and use credit wisely**. Stay committed, stay disciplined, and watch your financial situation improve dramatically.

Chapter 3: Eliminating Debt: Strategies for a Debt-Free Life

Debt is one of the biggest obstacles to financial freedom. It can limit your opportunities, drain your wealth, and keep you trapped in a cycle of financial stress. However, with the right strategy, anyone can break free from debt and build a stable, prosperous financial future.

This chapter will guide you through a step-by-step approach to eliminating debt, understanding different types of debt, avoiding common pitfalls, and creating a sustainable plan to remain debt-free.

3.1 Understanding Debt: The Good, The Bad, and The Ugly

Not all debt is bad. Some forms of debt can help build wealth, while others can quickly become financial burdens.

Good Debt vs. Bad Debt

◈ **Good Debt:** Helps you build assets, generate income, or improve your financial future.
Examples:

- **Mortgage Loans:** Owning a home can build equity over time.
- **Student Loans:** Education can lead to higher earnings, making it a worthwhile investment.
- **Business Loans:** When used wisely, debt can help grow a profitable business.

◈ **Bad Debt:** High-interest debt that does not contribute to wealth-building and often leads to financial strain.
Examples:

- **Credit Card Debt:** High-interest rates can spiral out of control.
- **Personal Loans for Unnecessary Spending:** Borrowing for vacations, gadgets, or shopping adds to financial stress.
- **Payday Loans:** Extremely high-interest loans that trap borrowers in cycles of repayment.

Understanding the difference between good and bad debt helps you make smarter borrowing decisions.

3.2 The True Cost of Debt: How It Drains Your Wealth

Debt is not just the amount you owe—it's the interest you pay over time that makes it dangerous.

How Interest Works Against You

The longer you take to pay off a loan, the more interest accumulates. For example, if you have a **$5,000 credit card balance** with a **20% interest rate**, making only the minimum payments could take **more than 15 years** to pay off and cost you over **$10,000** in total.

This is why getting rid of debt as quickly as possible is essential to financial success.

3.3 Step-by-Step Guide to Becoming Debt-Free

Eliminating debt requires a clear plan and disciplined execution. Here's a proven strategy to help you get started:

Step 1: List All Your Debts

Create a full inventory of what you owe, including:

- The total balance
- Interest rate
- Minimum monthly payment
- Due date

Use a simple spreadsheet or a debt tracker app to organize your debts.

Step 2: Prioritize Your Debts Using the Best Payoff Strategy
There are two effective debt repayment methods:
1. The Snowball Method (Quick Wins for Motivation)

- Focus on paying off the **smallest debt first** while making minimum payments on the others.
- Once the smallest debt is paid off, roll that payment into the next smallest debt.
- Repeat the process, gaining momentum as each debt is eliminated.

◈ **Best for:** People who need motivation and small wins to stay on track.

2. The Avalanche Method (Saves the Most Money on Interest)

- Focus on paying off the **highest-interest debt first** while making minimum payments on the others.
- Once the highest-interest debt is gone, move to the next highest.
- This strategy reduces the total amount of interest paid over time.

◈ **Best for:** People who want to save the most money in the long run.

Step 3: Cut Expenses to Free Up Extra Cash

The faster you can eliminate debt, the better. Reducing unnecessary expenses allows you to put more money toward paying off balances.

Ways to Free Up Money for Debt Repayment:

- **Cancel subscriptions** (streaming services, magazines, gyms).
- **Cook at home** instead of eating out.
- **Negotiate lower bills** for phone, insurance, and utilities.
- **Use public transportation** instead of driving everywhere.
- **Pause luxury spending** (vacations, designer clothes, unnecessary gadgets).

Every extra dollar saved should go toward reducing debt.

Step 4: Increase Your Income for Faster Debt Payoff

Boosting your earnings speeds up the debt-free journey.

Ways to Increase Income:

- **Start a Side Hustle** – Freelancing, selling digital products, or driving for Uber.
- **Ask for a Raise** – If you have been performing well at work, negotiate a higher salary.
- **Sell Unused Items** – Clothes, electronics, furniture—turn clutter into cash.
- **Rent Out Assets** – If you have extra space, rent it out on Airbnb.

Step 5: Automate Payments & Avoid Late Fees

Set up **automatic payments** to ensure you never miss a due date. Late fees add unnecessary costs and damage your credit score.

3.4 How to Avoid Common Debt Pitfalls

◈ Pitfall #1: Making Only Minimum Payments

- Paying only the minimum keeps you trapped in debt for years due to accumulating interest.

◈ Pitfall #2: Taking on New Debt While Paying Off Old Debt

- Do not open new credit lines while trying to eliminate debt.

◈ Pitfall #3: Using Debt Consolidation Without a Plan

- While consolidation can simplify payments, it does not solve the root problem of overspending.

◈ Pitfall #4: Ignoring Your Credit Score

- A low credit score can make borrowing more expensive in the future. Pay on time and keep balances low.

3.5 Staying Debt-Free for Life

Once you eliminate debt, the next step is **staying debt-free**.

Tips to Avoid Falling Back Into Debt:

◈ **Build an Emergency Fund:** Save at least **3-6 months' worth of expenses** so you don't rely on credit cards for emergencies.

◈ **Use Cash or Debit for Daily Spending:** Avoid unnecessary credit card use.

◈ **Set a Budget and Stick to It:** Continue tracking expenses even after becoming debt-free.

◈ **Invest Instead of Borrowing:** Grow your wealth through investments rather than taking on debt.

◈ **Live Below Your Means:** Avoid lifestyle inflation by keeping expenses lower than income.

Financial freedom is about **control**—when you master your money, debt will never control you again.

3.6 Conclusion: Take Control of Your Financial Future

Debt elimination is not just about paying off balances—it's about **changing your mindset** and adopting smart financial habits that keep you out of debt forever.

By **understanding your debt, choosing the right repayment strategy, cutting expenses, increasing income, and avoiding common pitfalls**, you can create a debt-free future and take full control of your financial destiny.

Your next step is to **start building wealth** by investing wisely and making your money work for you.

The journey to financial independence starts with eliminating debt—your future self will thank you for it.

Chapter 4: The Psychology of Money: Changing Your Mindset

Money is not just about numbers, budgets, and bank accounts—it is deeply tied to psychology. The way you think about money determines how you manage it, how you invest it, and ultimately, whether you achieve financial freedom. If you want to build lasting wealth, you must first develop a healthy financial mindset.

This chapter will explore the psychology of money, how beliefs shape financial behavior, and how to shift your mindset to achieve financial independence. By understanding the emotions and mental habits tied to wealth, you can take control of your financial future and **start building wealth by investing wisely and making your money work for you**.

4.1 The Power of Financial Mindset

Your thoughts about money influence your financial success more than your income. Many people with high salaries still struggle with debt, while others with modest earnings accumulate wealth over time. The key difference? **Mindset.**

There are two primary money mindsets:

1. The Scarcity Mindset (Keeping You Stuck)

People with a scarcity mindset believe there is never enough money. They focus on limitations, fear losing money, and struggle to grow wealth.

Signs of a scarcity mindset:

- Always worrying about money.
- Feeling guilty about spending.
- Avoiding investments due to fear of loss.
- Living paycheck to paycheck despite earning well.

2. The Abundance Mindset (Building Wealth)

People with an abundance mindset see money as a tool that can be grown, managed, and used to create opportunities. They focus on making money work for them instead of fearing it.

Signs of an abundance mindset:

- Viewing money as a tool for growth.
- Taking calculated risks to grow wealth.
- Looking for multiple income streams.
- Understanding that money is infinite, not limited.

To shift from scarcity to abundance, you must **reprogram your beliefs about money** and develop financial habits that align with long-term wealth-building.

4.2 Identifying & Overcoming Limiting Money Beliefs

Many financial struggles come from childhood money beliefs passed down through family, culture, or past experiences. If you believe that "money is evil" or "rich people are greedy," your subconscious will **sabotage** your efforts to accumulate wealth.

Common Money Beliefs That Hold You Back:

◈ **"I'm just bad with money."** → Money management is a skill anyone can learn.

◈ **"Investing is risky—I'll lose everything."** → Not investing is the bigger risk, as inflation erodes savings.

◈ **"You have to work hard to get rich."** → Working smart (leveraging passive income and investments) is more important than just working hard.

◈ **"Wealth is only for the lucky or privileged."** → Many self-made millionaires started with nothing but changed their mindset and strategy.

Reprogramming Your Money Mindset:

◈ **Practice Gratitude:** Focus on what you have rather than what you lack.

◈ **Surround Yourself with Financially Smart People:** Learn from those who manage money well.

◈ **Develop a Growth Mindset:** Believe you can learn new financial skills and improve.

◈ **Visualize Your Financial Goals:** Picture your future self as financially independent.

Your mindset determines your financial habits, which ultimately shape your wealth. By shifting limiting beliefs, you unlock the ability to **make smarter financial decisions and start growing your money.**

4.3 Understanding Emotional Spending & Financial Habits

Money is deeply emotional. People often make financial decisions based on **feelings rather than logic**, which can lead to bad spending habits.

Common Emotional Spending Triggers:

1. **Stress & Anxiety** – Using shopping as a coping mechanism.
2. **Boredom** – Spending money to fill emotional voids.
3. **FOMO (Fear of Missing Out)** – Buying things you don't need to keep up with others.
4. **Guilt & Shame** – Overspending to make up for past financial mistakes.
5. **Instant Gratification** – Choosing short-term pleasure over long-term financial security.

How to Control Emotional Spending:

- **Pause Before You Purchase:** Wait 24 hours before making non-essential purchases.
- **Create a Fun Budget:** Allow yourself guilt-free spending within limits.
- **Use Cash or Debit:** Avoid credit cards for impulse buys.
- **Set Clear Financial Goals:** When you have a goal, you are less likely to waste money.

By recognizing emotional triggers, you can take control of your financial behavior and **redirect spending toward building wealth instead of unnecessary purchases.**

4.4 The Wealth-Building Mindset: Making Money Work for You

The wealthy don't just work for money—they **make money work for them**. This shift in thinking is what separates financially successful people from those who struggle.

The Wealthy Follow These Principles:

⟐ **They Focus on Assets, Not Just Income:** They invest in things that grow in value (stocks, real estate, businesses).

⟐ **They Create Passive Income:** They earn money even while sleeping.

⟐ **They Leverage Time and Compound Interest:** They start investing early and let their money grow.

⟐ **They Avoid Lifestyle Inflation:** As their income increases, they don't overspend.

Instead of thinking **"How can I make more money?"** ask:

⟐ **"How can I make my money work for me?"**

4.5 Investing Wisely: The Key to Long-Term Wealth

Once you master your financial mindset, it's time to start building wealth. **Investing is the single most powerful way to grow money over time.**

Why Investing Matters:

- **Beats Inflation:** Savings accounts lose value over time due to inflation. Investing grows your money faster.
- **Generates Passive Income:** Stocks, real estate, and businesses can pay you without daily work.
- **Creates Financial Security:** Investments provide long-term financial stability.

Best Ways to Start Investing:

◈ **Stock Market:** Buy shares of companies, ETFs, or index funds.
◈ **Real Estate:** Purchase rental properties or invest in REITs.
◈ **Starting a Business:** Entrepreneurship can create financial independence.
◈ **Retirement Accounts (401k, IRA):** Invest in tax-advantaged accounts for future wealth.

Investing early allows you to benefit from compound interest—which means your money earns money over time.

4.6 The Power of Compound Interest: Turning Small Investments into Wealth

◈ Albert Einstein called compound interest "the eighth wonder of the world."

Compound interest means **your money earns interest, and that interest also earns interest over time**.

Example of Compound Growth:

If you invest **$500 per month** at a **7% annual return**, after:

- **10 years = $86,000**
- **20 years = $247,000**
- **30 years = $566,000**

Even small investments **grow exponentially over time**. The earlier you start, the more wealth you build.

4.7 Developing a Long-Term Wealth Plan

Shifting your money mindset is the first step—but building real wealth requires action.

Steps to Create a Wealth Plan:

1. **Define Your Financial Goals:** Retirement, passive income, homeownership, travel, or entrepreneurship.
2. **Budget with Investing in Mind:** Allocate at least **20% of income** toward wealth-building.
3. **Automate Investments:** Set up automatic contributions to stock portfolios or retirement accounts.
4. **Avoid High-Interest Debt:** Stay debt-free so you can invest more.
5. **Reinvest Profits:** Let money grow rather than withdrawing early.

With the right mindset and strategy, **anyone can achieve financial independence**.

4.8 Conclusion: Your Wealth Starts in Your Mind

Changing your financial future starts with **changing how you think about money**.

By:

⟐ **Shifting from a scarcity to an abundance mindset**
⟐ **Recognizing emotional spending habits**
⟐ **Understanding how to make money work for you**
⟐ **Investing early and consistently**

You position yourself for **lifelong financial success.**

The next step in your journey is learning **how to generate multiple income streams and maximize your earning potential**.

Your wealth begins today. Are you ready to take control? ⟐

Chapter 5: Passive Income – Making Money While You Sleep

One of the greatest secrets to financial freedom is learning how to earn money without constantly trading your time for it. Passive income is the key to wealth-building and financial independence, allowing you to generate money while you sleep, travel, or pursue your passions.

In this chapter, we will explore **how to generate multiple income streams, maximize your earning potential, and create a sustainable system that works for you**. By leveraging passive income strategies, you can break free from the cycle of paycheck-to-paycheck living and design a life of financial security and abundance.

5.1 What is Passive Income?

Passive income is money earned with little to no daily effort after the initial work is done. Unlike a traditional job, where you exchange time for money, passive income allows you to **build assets that generate continuous revenue over time**.

Passive Income vs. Active Income

◈ **Active Income** – Requires direct effort (e.g., salary, hourly wages, freelancing).

◈ **Passive Income** – Generates revenue automatically with minimal ongoing effort (e.g., investments, rental income, digital products).

The **wealthy focus on passive income streams** because they create financial freedom, whereas relying solely on active income keeps you trapped in the cycle of working just to pay bills.

5.2 The Importance of Multiple Income Streams

One income stream is risky. If you only have one source of income (like a job), losing it can cause financial disaster. The most financially successful people **build multiple streams of income** so they always have money flowing in from different sources.

Benefits of Multiple Income Streams:

◈ **More Financial Security** – If one stream dries up, others keep money flowing.

◈ **Wealth Accumulation** – Passive income allows you to reinvest and grow your assets.

◈ **Time Freedom** – Less dependence on traditional 9-to-5 jobs.

◈ **Retirement Preparation** – Passive income ensures financial stability in later years.

The goal is to **replace your active income with passive income**, so eventually, you can live comfortably without needing a job.

5.3 Types of Passive Income & How to Get Started

1. Dividend Stocks (Investing for Passive Growth)

Dividend stocks pay shareholders a portion of company profits. Investing in these allows you to earn money regularly without selling stocks.

◈ **How to Start:**

- Open a brokerage account (e.g., Fidelity, Vanguard, Robinhood).
- Invest in **dividend-paying companies or ETFs**.
- Reinvest dividends to **compound your wealth** over time.

◈ **Potential Earnings:** $100–$5,000+ per month (depending on investment size).

2. Real Estate Investments (Earning Rental Income)

Owning rental properties is a classic way to generate passive income. If done right, real estate can provide long-term financial stability.

◈ **How to Start:**

- Buy rental property in high-demand areas.
- Rent it out to tenants and collect monthly income.
- Use property management services to make it **truly passive**.

◈ **Potential Earnings:** $500–$5,000+ per month per property.

No money for real estate? Consider **Real Estate Investment Trusts (REITs)**, which let you invest in real estate without owning property.

3. Creating & Selling Digital Products

Digital products are one of the best passive income streams because **they require no physical inventory** and can be sold repeatedly.

◈ **Examples of Digital Products:**

- Ebooks
- Online courses
- Stock photos
- Digital art/printables
- Software or apps

◈ **How to Start:**

- Identify a topic you have expertise in.
- Create a **high-quality digital product** (use platforms like Canva, Teachable, or Gumroad).
- Sell on **Etsy, Amazon, or your website**.

◈ **Potential Earnings:** $1,000–$50,000+ per month (scalable).

4. Affiliate Marketing (Earning Commissions on Sales)

Affiliate marketing allows you to earn commissions by promoting other companies' products. It is **low-risk and requires no upfront investment**.

◈ **How to Start:**

- Join affiliate programs (Amazon Associates, ClickBank, CJ Affiliate).
- Promote products through **a blog, YouTube, or social media**.
- Earn commissions on every sale made through your links.

◈ **Potential Earnings:** $100–$50,000+ per month (depends on traffic).

◈ **Example:** A food blogger recommending kitchen gadgets on Amazon earns a commission whenever someone buys through their links.

5. Selling Print-on-Demand Products

Print-on-demand (POD) lets you sell custom-designed items **without handling inventory**.

◈ **Examples of POD Products:**

- T-shirts
- Mugs
- Hoodies
- Phone cases
- Stickers

◈ **How to Start:**

- Create designs using **Canva or Photoshop**.
- Upload them to POD platforms like **Teespring, Redbubble, or Printful**.
- The platform **handles production and shipping**—you earn passive income from every sale.

◈ **Potential Earnings:** $500–$10,000+ per month.

6. Writing a Book or Self-Publishing

Publishing a book allows you to **earn royalties indefinitely**.

◈ **How to Start:**

- Write a **nonfiction book, novel, or guide**.
- Publish on Amazon Kindle Direct Publishing (KDP), Apple Books, or Kobo.
- Market the book through **social media, blogs, and email lists**.

◈ **Potential Earnings:** $1,000–$100,000+ per month (depending on sales).

◈ **Tip:** Focus on evergreen topics that people will always buy (e.g., self-help, finance, business, health).

7. YouTube Automation (Monetizing Content Passively)

YouTube pays creators through **ads, sponsorships, and affiliate marketing**.

◈ **How to Start:**

- Create videos about a niche (finance, tech, health, etc.).
- Monetize with **YouTube Partner Program**.
- Outsource video creation for **a fully passive YouTube business**.

◈ **Potential Earnings:** $1,000–$100,000+ per month (scalable).

◈ **Example:** A **motivational YouTube channel** using AI voiceovers and stock footage can generate ad revenue without filming original content.

5.4 Scaling Your Passive Income Streams

Once you have one stream of passive income, the goal is to **scale it up** and diversify into multiple streams.

◈ **Steps to Scale:**

1. **Automate Processes** – Use tools to schedule content, automate emails, and outsource tasks.
2. **Reinvest Profits** – Take earnings from one stream and invest in others (e.g., using affiliate income to buy dividend stocks).
3. **Expand to New Markets** – Translate books into different languages, sell courses globally, or target new audiences.

◈ **Example:** A YouTube creator earning $5,000/month reinvests into real estate and stocks, compounding their wealth exponentially.

5.5 Achieving Financial Freedom with Passive Income

Once your **passive income exceeds your expenses**, you achieve financial freedom.

Final Steps to Financial Independence:

◈ Build at least **3+ income streams**.
◈ Reinvest profits to **accelerate growth**.
◈ Continue learning & adapting to **new opportunities**.
◈ Maintain **financial discipline** (avoid lifestyle inflation).

5.6 Conclusion: Your Path to Passive Wealth Starts Now

Creating passive income **takes effort upfront**, but once it's set up, it generates money without constant work. The sooner you start, the faster you can **escape the 9-to-5 grind** and create **true financial independence**.

mastering investing strategies to maximize wealth and create lasting financial security is your next step.

Your journey to financial freedom starts today. What passive income stream will you build first? ◈

Chapter 6: Smart Investments for Beginners

Investing is one of the most powerful tools for building wealth and achieving financial security. It allows your money to grow exponentially over time, freeing you from the limitations of relying solely on active income. However, many beginners avoid investing due to fear, lack of knowledge, or past financial mistakes.

This chapter will serve as a **comprehensive guide to mastering investing strategies to maximize wealth and create lasting financial security**. By the end, you'll understand how to start investing, minimize risks, and build a strong portfolio that works for you.

6.1 Why Investing is Essential for Financial Freedom

If you want to build wealth, **saving alone is not enough**. Inflation slowly erodes the value of money, making it essential to put your money to work through smart investments.

Benefits of Investing:

◈ **Beats Inflation** – Investing helps your money grow faster than inflation, maintaining its value.

◈ **Generates Passive Income** – Certain investments, like dividend stocks and real estate, provide ongoing income.

◈ **Builds Long-Term Wealth** – Compound interest and reinvestment lead to exponential financial growth.

◈ **Provides Financial Security** – Well-planned investments reduce financial stress and prepare you for retirement.

By **starting early and investing consistently**, you set yourself up for a secure financial future.

6.2 Understanding Investment Basics

Before diving into investment strategies, you must understand the key investment concepts that will help you make informed decisions.

1. Risk vs. Reward

Every investment carries some level of risk. Generally:

- **Higher risk = Higher potential returns** (e.g., stocks, crypto).
- **Lower risk = Lower returns** (e.g., bonds, savings accounts).

Successful investing is about **balancing risk** to achieve long-term financial growth.

2. The Power of Compound Interest

Compound interest allows your investments to grow exponentially over time.

◈ **Example:** If you invest $500/month at a 7% return:

- **After 10 years** → $86,000
- **After 20 years** → $247,000
- **After 30 years** → $566,000

Starting **early** and **investing consistently** allows your money to work for you.

3. Diversification: The Key to Reducing Risk

Never put all your money into one investment. Diversifying across different assets protects your portfolio from market downturns.

◈ **Rule of Thumb:** "Don't put all your eggs in one basket."

6.3 Types of Investments and How to Get Started

There are many ways to invest, and choosing the right option depends on your financial goals and risk tolerance.

1. Stock Market Investing (Owning a Piece of Companies)

◈ **What It Is:** Buying shares in companies that grow in value over time.

◈ **Best For:** Long-term wealth building.

◈ **Ways to Invest in Stocks:**

◈ **Individual Stocks:** Buy shares of companies like Apple, Amazon, or Tesla.

◈ **Index Funds & ETFs:** Invest in a bundle of stocks (e.g., S&P 500) for automatic diversification.

◈ **Dividend Stocks:** Invest in companies that pay you regularly (e.g., Coca-Cola, Johnson & Johnson).

◈ **How to Start:**

1. Open a brokerage account (Fidelity, Vanguard, Robinhood).
2. Invest in **index funds or ETFs** to reduce risk.
3. Hold investments long-term (avoid panic selling).

◈ **Potential Earnings:** 7-10% annual return on average.

2. Real Estate Investing (Building Wealth Through Property)

◈ **What It Is:** Buying property to rent out or sell for a profit.
◈ **Best For:** Generating passive income and long-term appreciation.
◈ **Ways to Invest in Real Estate:**
◈ **Rental Properties:** Earn monthly rent while property value increases.
◈ **House Flipping:** Buy, renovate, and sell homes for profit.
◈ **Real Estate Investment Trusts (REITs):** Invest in real estate **without owning property**.
◈ **How to Start:**

1. Save for a down payment (typically 20% of property value).
2. Research **high-demand rental markets**.
3. If you don't want to manage properties, invest in **REITs**.

◈ **Potential Earnings:** $500–$5,000+ per month per property.

3. Bonds & Fixed-Income Investments (Lower Risk, Steady Growth)

◈ **What It Is:** Lending money to the government or corporations in exchange for interest.
◈ **Best For:** Conservative investors seeking stable returns.
◈ **Types of Bonds:**
◈ **Government Bonds:** Low-risk investments backed by the government (e.g., U.S. Treasury Bonds).
◈ **Corporate Bonds:** Companies pay you interest over time
◈ **How to Start:**

1. Buy bonds through your brokerage account.
2. Hold them for **steady, guaranteed returns**.

◈ **Potential Earnings:** 2-5% annual return.

4. Cryptocurrency Investing (High-Risk, High-Reward)

◈ **What It Is:** Digital assets like Bitcoin and Ethereum that grow in value over time.

◈ **Best For:** Investors willing to take higher risks for potential big returns.

◈ **How to Start:**

1. Use platforms like **Coinbase, Binance, or Kraken**.
2. Invest only **what you can afford to lose**.
3. Hold for the long term (avoid panic selling).

◈ **Potential Earnings:** Unpredictable—can be very high but also volatile.

5. Retirement Accounts (Secure Your Future)

◈ **What It Is:** Tax-advantaged investment accounts to grow wealth for retirement.

◈ **Best For:** Anyone wanting **financial security in old age**.

◈ **Best Retirement Accounts:**

◈ **401(k):** Employer-sponsored plan (often with matching contributions).

◈ **IRA & Roth IRA:** Tax-free or tax-deferred investment growth.

◈ **How to Start:**

1. If your employer offers a **401(k) match**, contribute **at least up to the match** (free money!).
2. Open a **Roth IRA** for tax-free retirement withdrawals.

◈ **Potential Earnings:** $1M+ if you start early and invest consistently.

6.4 Smart Investment Strategies for Beginners

1. Start Small & Invest Consistently

◈ **Strategy:** Invest a set amount each month (Dollar-Cost Averaging).

◈ **Example:** Investing $200/month for 30 years in the S&P 500 can grow to **$500,000+**.

2. Use the 80/20 Rule (Passive vs. Active Investing)

◈ **Strategy:**

- **80% in safe, passive investments** (Index Funds, ETFs, Bonds).
- **20% in high-risk investments** (Crypto, Individual Stocks).

3. Avoid Common Beginner Mistakes

◈ **Panic Selling** – Don't sell investments during market downturns.

◈ **Chasing Quick Profits** – Stick to long-term strategies.

◈ **Ignoring Fees** – Choose low-cost index funds to maximize returns.

6.5 The Path to Financial Security Through Investing

◈ **Investing is a long-term game**—the key to wealth-building is patience and consistency.

◈ **Start with what you can afford**—even small amounts compound over time.

◈ **Diversify and automate** your investments for steady, stress-free growth.

The best time to start investing was yesterday—the second-best time is **today**.

Are you ready to build your future wealth? ◈

Chapter 7: Side Hustles and Entrepreneurship

Building wealth is not just about saving and investing—it's also about increasing your income. Side hustles and entrepreneurship provide opportunities to boost your earnings, diversify income streams, and achieve financial independence faster. Whether you want extra income to pay off debt, invest, or transition into full-time business ownership, side hustles and entrepreneurship can be powerful wealth-building tools.

In this chapter, we'll explore **how to start profitable side hustles, build a successful business, and protect your wealth through financial planning, insurance, and smart risk management**.

7.1 Why Side Hustles and Entrepreneurship Matter

Having a single source of income is risky. If you lose your job, your financial security disappears overnight. That's why creating multiple income streams through side hustles or entrepreneurship is essential for long-term wealth and stability.

Benefits of Side Hustles and Entrepreneurship:

◈ **Increases Income** – More money means faster debt repayment, savings growth, and investment opportunities.

◈ **Provides Financial Security** – Reduces dependence on a single paycheck.

◈ **Gives You Freedom** – Running your own business can allow you to work on your terms.

◈ **Creates Passive Income** – Some businesses generate money even while you sleep.

The goal is to **turn a side hustle into a business that works for you** and protects your financial future.

7.2 Finding the Right Side Hustle

Not all side hustles are created equal. The best ones align with your skills, time availability, and income goals.

1. Time-Based Side Hustles (Active Income)

These require direct work, meaning you trade time for money.

◈ **Examples:**

- **Freelancing** (Writing, Graphic Design, Web Development)
- **Rideshare & Delivery** (Uber, DoorDash, Instacart)
- **Tutoring & Coaching** (Online courses, Test Prep, Business Consulting)
- **Pet Sitting & House Sitting** (Rover, Trusted Housesitters)

◈ **How to Start:**

1. Identify a skill or service you can offer.
2. Use platforms like **Upwork, Fiverr, or TaskRabbit** to find clients.
3. Set competitive rates and provide high-quality work.

◈ **Potential Earnings:** $500–$5,000/month.

2. Digital Side Hustles (Passive & Scalable Income)
These can generate money with minimal ongoing effort.
◈ **Examples:**

- **Print-on-Demand (POD)** (Selling custom T-shirts, mugs, and stickers)
- **Affiliate Marketing** (Earning commissions by promoting products)
- **Selling Digital Products** (Ebooks, Online Courses, Templates)
- **Stock Photography & Videos** (Selling on Shutterstock, Adobe Stock)

◈ **How to Start:**

1. Create valuable digital products or content.
2. Use platforms like **Etsy, Gumroad, or Teespring** to sell.
3. Automate marketing through blogs, YouTube, or social media.

◈ **Potential Earnings:** $1,000–$50,000/month.

3. E-commerce & Reselling

Selling physical products can be a profitable side business.

⟐ **Examples:**

- **Dropshipping** (Selling products without holding inventory)
- **Amazon FBA** (Selling products on Amazon)
- **Flipping Items** (Buying low, selling high on eBay, Facebook Marketplace)

⟐ **How to Start:**

1. Choose a niche (electronics, clothing, handmade items).
2. Source products (Alibaba, local thrift stores, wholesale suppliers).
3. Sell on **Amazon, eBay, Shopify, or Etsy**.

⟐ **Potential Earnings:** $500–$100,000/month.

7.3 Turning a Side Hustle into a Full-Time Business

A successful side hustle can grow into a profitable business. To make this transition, you need a **scalable strategy**.

Steps to Grow a Side Hustle into a Business:

⟐ **1. Establish a Strong Brand**

- Choose a memorable business name.
- Create a professional website and social media presence.

⟐ **2. Automate & Scale**

- Outsource tasks (hire freelancers or virtual assistants).
- Use automation tools for marketing and customer service.

⟐ **3. Expand Your Revenue Streams**

- Sell products/services in multiple places.
- Create multiple sources of income within your business.

⟐ **4. Network & Build Relationships**

- Collaborate with influencers or business partners.
- Join entrepreneur communities and forums.

⟐ **Example:** A **freelance writer** can scale by hiring a team of writers, creating an online course, or offering premium consulting services.

7.4 Protecting Your Wealth: Financial Planning, Insurance, and Risk Management

As you build wealth through side hustles and entrepreneurship, **protecting your financial success** is just as important as making money.

1. Financial Planning for Entrepreneurs

Unlike employees with steady paychecks, entrepreneurs must create **a financial plan** to ensure stability.

◈ **Key Financial Planning Steps:**

◈ **Separate Personal & Business Finances:** Open a dedicated business bank account.

◈ **Build an Emergency Fund:** Save at least **6-12 months** of expenses.

◈ **Plan for Taxes:** Set aside **30% of earnings** for taxes and deductions.

◈ **Invest for Retirement:** Open a **Solo 401(k) or SEP IRA** to grow tax-free wealth.

2. Business & Personal Insurance

◈ **Why It Matters:** Unexpected events (lawsuits, accidents, health issues) can ruin finances without proper insurance.

◈ **Essential Insurance for Entrepreneurs:**

◈ **Health Insurance:** Prevents medical bills from draining savings.

◈ **Business Liability Insurance:** Protects against lawsuits.

◈ **Disability Insurance:** Provides income if you're unable to work.

◈ **Life Insurance:** Ensures your family is financially secure.

◈ **Example:** A business owner with **liability insurance** is protected if a customer sues over a faulty product.

3. Smart Risk Management Strategies

◈ **How to Reduce Financial Risk as an Entrepreneur:**

◈ **Diversify Your Income:** Don't rely on one revenue stream—spread your earnings across multiple ventures.

◈ **Use Contracts for Business Deals:** Protect yourself legally when working with clients or partners.

◈ **Limit Debt Exposure:** Avoid overleveraging—grow sustainably.

◈ **Save & Reinvest Profits:** Always reinvest a portion of earnings into business growth.

7.5 Achieving Financial Independence Through Entrepreneurship

Side hustles and entrepreneurship are not just about making extra money—they're about **creating a lifestyle of financial freedom**. The key is **starting small, growing steadily, and protecting your wealth** as you scale.

Steps to Financial Independence Through Business:

1◈ **Start with a Side Hustle** – Choose something aligned with your skills and goals.

2◈ **Scale to a Business** – Build a brand, automate, and increase income streams.

3◈ **Protect Your Wealth** – Use smart financial planning and insurance.

4◈ **Reinvest for Growth** – Put profits into new opportunities for passive income.

◈ **Example:** A graphic designer making $2,000/month freelancing expands by selling templates, launching an online course, and hiring a team—scaling earnings to **$20,000+/month**.

7.6 Conclusion: Your Journey to Wealth Begins Today

Entrepreneurship is one of the fastest paths to financial independence—but only if done **strategically and with financial protection in place**.

◈ **Choose a profitable side hustle or business model.**

◈ **Scale your business while minimizing risk.**

◈ **Use financial planning, insurance, and investments to secure your wealth.**

Are you ready to turn your side hustle into a financial empire? ◈

Chapter 8: Mastering Taxes – How to Maximize Savings

Taxes are one of the largest expenses most people face in their lifetime. Whether you're an employee, a freelancer, or a business owner, understanding how taxes work is essential to maximizing savings, increasing your take-home income, and securing long-term financial stability.

In this chapter, we will explore **how to legally reduce tax liabilities, take advantage of deductions, and implement smart tax strategies that support wealth-building and retirement planning**. By learning how to navigate taxes effectively, you can keep more of your hard-earned money and invest it wisely for a secure financial future.

8.1 Understanding How Taxes Work

Before diving into tax-saving strategies, it's essential to understand the basics of how taxes are calculated and what types of taxes impact your income and investments.

1. Types of Taxes You Pay

◈ **Income Tax** – Tax on wages, salaries, and business income.

◈ **Self-Employment Tax** – Social Security & Medicare taxes for freelancers and entrepreneurs.

◈ **Capital Gains Tax** – Tax on profits from selling stocks, real estate, or other investments.

◈ **Property Tax** – Tax on owned real estate.

◈ **Sales Tax** – Tax on goods and services purchased.

◈ **Estate & Inheritance Tax** – Tax on inherited assets (varies by state).

◈ **Why It Matters:** Understanding these taxes helps you identify legal ways to **minimize tax liabilities** and maximize savings.

8.2 How to Reduce Taxable Income (Legally!)

The government provides **numerous tax breaks** to help individuals and businesses reduce their tax burden. By using **deductions, credits, and tax-advantaged accounts**, you can significantly lower your taxable income.

1. Maximize Tax Deductions

Tax deductions reduce the amount of income that gets taxed, lowering the overall tax bill.

◈ **Common Deductions for Employees & Freelancers:**

◈ **Retirement Contributions (401k, IRA, SEP IRA)** – Contributions reduce taxable income.

◈ **Health Savings Account (HSA) Contributions** – Tax-free savings for medical expenses.

◈ **Home Office Deduction** – If you work from home, you can deduct rent, utilities, and internet.

◈ **Business Expenses** – Freelancers and entrepreneurs can deduct costs like equipment, software, and marketing.

◈ **Educational Expenses** – Tuition, certifications, and training can be deducted.

◈ **Example:** If you earn $60,000 and contribute $6,000 to an IRA, your taxable income drops to $54,000—saving you **hundreds or thousands in taxes.**

2. Take Advantage of Tax Credits

Tax credits directly reduce the amount of taxes owed, dollar-for-dollar.

◈ **Common Tax Credits:**

◈ **Earned Income Tax Credit (EITC)** – Helps low-to-moderate-income earners.

◈ **Child Tax Credit** – $2,000 per child under 17.

◈ **Education Credits (Lifetime Learning, American Opportunity)** – Reduces costs of higher education.

◈ **Energy-Efficient Home Credits** – Save on solar panels, energy-efficient appliances, and home improvements.

◈ **Example:** If you owe $3,000 in taxes but qualify for a $2,000 tax credit, your tax bill drops to **$1,000**.

8.3 Retirement Planning & Tax-Advantaged Accounts

One of the best ways to **reduce taxes while building long-term wealth** is through retirement accounts.

1. Tax-Advantaged Retirement Accounts

◈ **Best Accounts for Tax Savings & Retirement Security:**

◈ **401(k) or 403(b) (Employer-Sponsored Plans)** – Contributions are tax-deductible, reducing taxable income.

◈ **Traditional IRA** – Contributions reduce taxable income; taxes are paid upon withdrawal in retirement.

◈ **Roth IRA** – No immediate tax deduction, but withdrawals in retirement are **100% tax-free**.

◈ **SEP IRA or Solo 401(k)** – For freelancers/business owners; higher contribution limits allow for bigger tax deductions.

◈ **Example:** Contributing **$10,000** to a 401(k) reduces taxable income by the same amount, **saving you thousands in taxes** while growing wealth for retirement.

2. Required Minimum Distributions (RMDs)

At **age** 73, the IRS requires withdrawals from traditional retirement accounts. Planning ahead helps avoid unnecessary taxes and penalties.

8.4 Smart Tax Strategies for Investors & Business Owners

Beyond retirement savings, there are **powerful investment and business tax strategies** that maximize wealth.

1. Tax-Efficient Investing

◈ **Ways to Reduce Investment Taxes:**

◈ **Hold Investments for Over a Year** – Lower long-term capital gains tax (0–20%) vs. short-term (taxed as ordinary income).

◈ **Use Tax-Advantaged Accounts (Roth IRA, 401(k))** – Investment growth is tax-free or tax-deferred.

◈ **Harvest Tax Losses** – Sell losing stocks to offset taxable gains.

◈ **Invest in Municipal Bonds** – Tax-free interest income.

◈ **Example:** Selling a stock held for **over a year** is taxed at a **lower rate** than selling it early.

2. Tax Strategies for Entrepreneurs & Freelancers

◈ **How Business Owners Can Save on Taxes:**

◈ **Deduct Business Expenses** – Write off office supplies, travel, and marketing.

◈ **Use S-Corp Status** – Reduces self-employment tax.

◈ **Hire Family Members** – Pay wages to family and shift income to lower tax brackets.

◈ **Max Out Business Retirement Plans (Solo 401(k), SEP IRA)** – Reduces taxable business income.

◈ **Example:** A freelancer earning $100,000 can deduct **home office expenses, business travel, and equipment costs**, reducing taxable income **by thousands**.

8.5 How to Plan for Taxes & Avoid Common Mistakes

◈ **Key Tax Planning Tips:**

◈ **Estimate Taxes Quarterly** – If self-employed, make quarterly tax payments to avoid penalties.

◈ **Use a Tax Professional** – An accountant can identify overlooked tax deductions.

◈ **Keep Detailed Records** – Store receipts, invoices, and financial documents to support deductions.

◈ **Set Aside Money for Taxes** – Entrepreneurs should allocate **30% of earnings** to avoid surprises.

◈ **Common Tax Mistakes to Avoid:**

◈ Not filing on time (leads to penalties).

◈ Forgetting deductions (leaves money on the table).

◈ Not contributing to retirement accounts (missed tax benefits).

◈ Overpaying taxes (due to lack of tax planning).

8.6 How Taxes Fit into Long-Term Financial Security

Taxes should be viewed as part of **a larger wealth strategy**. By using smart tax planning, you can **keep more money, grow investments, and achieve financial independence faster**.

The Wealth Triangle: Taxes, Investments, and Protection

◈ **Minimize Taxes** – Use deductions, credits, and tax-advantaged accounts.

◈ **Invest Wisely** – Keep more earnings invested for long-term growth.

◈ **Protect Wealth** – Use insurance and estate planning to secure financial stability.

◈ **Example:** A **business owner who contributes to retirement, invests in tax-free assets, and deducts business expenses** saves thousands in taxes while **building wealth faster**.

8.7 Conclusion: Master Your Taxes, Secure Your Wealth

Taxes don't have to be a burden—when understood and planned for, they become a **powerful tool for financial security and wealth creation**.

◈ **Maximize deductions & credits** to lower taxable income.
◈ **Invest in tax-advantaged retirement accounts** for long-term savings.
◈ **Use tax-efficient investment strategies** to grow wealth faster.
◈ **Plan ahead** to avoid tax mistakes and penalties.

◈ **Your tax strategy determines how much wealth you keep—are you ready to master it?** ◈

Chapter 9: The Importance of Multiple Income Streams

Relying on a single source of income is one of the biggest financial risks in today's world. With economic uncertainty, job automation, and market shifts, having multiple income streams is no longer a luxury—it's a necessity.

Wealthy individuals and financially successful people **diversify their income streams** to create financial stability, protect against unexpected hardships, and accelerate wealth-building. In this chapter, we'll explore **why multiple income streams are essential, the best types of income sources, and how to build and manage them effectively**.

9.1 Why You Need Multiple Income Streams

1. Protection Against Job Loss or Income Decline

If you rely solely on one job, losing it could leave you in financial ruin. Multiple income streams act as a safety net so you're never completely dependent on a single source of income.

2. Faster Wealth Accumulation

Having multiple streams allows you to **increase savings, invest more, and reach financial goals faster**. Instead of waiting years to build wealth through a paycheck, additional income sources can **accelerate your financial growth**.

3. More Financial Freedom and Flexibility

With several income streams, you have **greater control over your time and lifestyle**. It allows you to pursue passions, take risks, or even retire early.

4. Passive Income for Long-Term Security

Not all income should come from active work. Building **passive income streams** ensures that you continue earning even when you stop working.

5. Adapting to Changing Economies

Job markets evolve, industries change, and technology disrupts employment. Multiple income streams **reduce financial risk** and provide stability in uncertain times.

9.2 The Different Types of Income Streams

There are seven primary sources of income that millionaires and financially independent people use to build and maintain wealth.

1. Earned Income (Active Work) – Your Job or Business

This is the most common source of income—your salary, wages, or business revenue. While necessary, it's not enough to rely on alone.

⟐ **How to Optimize:**

⟐ Increase skills and negotiate higher pay.
⟐ Start a **side hustle** for additional income.
⟐ Turn expertise into **a consulting or coaching business**.

2. Profit Income – Selling Goods or Services

Profit income comes from selling something for more than it costs to produce.

⟐ **Examples:**

- Selling products online (Amazon, Shopify, Etsy).
- Flipping items (buying and reselling for profit).
- Running an e-commerce store.
- Selling digital products (ebooks, courses, templates).

⟐ **Potential Earnings:** $500–$100,000+/month (scalable).

3. Interest Income – Earnings from Lending Money

Interest income comes from lending money and earning a return over time.

⟐ **Examples:**

- High-yield savings accounts.
- Peer-to-peer lending platforms (LendingClub, Prosper).
- Bonds (government, corporate, or municipal).

⟐ **Tip:** Interest income is **low-risk and provides steady returns**, making it a great addition to any income portfolio.

⟐ **Potential Earnings:** 1-10% annual return.

4. Dividend Income – Getting Paid to Own Stocks

Dividend stocks pay investors **a share of company profits** regularly.

◈ **Best Dividend Stocks:**

- Coca-Cola
- Johnson & Johnson
- Procter & Gamble
- McDonald's

◈ **Tip:** Reinvest dividends to **compound wealth faster**.

◈ **Potential Earnings:** $100–$10,000/month (based on investment size).

5. Rental Income – Earning Money from Real Estate

Rental income provides **steady cash flow** and is one of the best passive income sources.

◈ **Ways to Earn Rental Income:**

◈ **Owning rental properties** (long-term tenants).

◈ **Short-term rentals** (Airbnb, vacation homes).

◈ **Real Estate Investment Trusts (REITs)** – Investing in real estate without owning property.

◈ **Potential Earnings:** $500–$5,000+/month per property.

6. Capital Gains – Making Money from Investments

Capital gains come from **buying assets at a lower price and selling them at a higher price**.

◈ **Examples:**

- Selling stocks, real estate, or businesses.
- Buying and selling cryptocurrency.
- Investing in collectibles (art, rare coins, vintage items).

◈ **Tip:** Holding investments for over a year reduces capital gains tax.

◈ **Potential Earnings:** Varies based on investment strategy.

7. Royalties & Licensing Income – Getting Paid for Intellectual Property

Royalties come from **creating something once and earning from it repeatedly**.

◈ **Examples:**

- Book royalties (self-publishing on Amazon KDP).
- Music royalties (Spotify, Apple Music).
- Licensing content, art, or software to businesses.
- Patents and trademarks.

◈ **Potential Earnings:** $100–$1,000,000+ (depends on demand).

9.3 How to Build Multiple Income Streams

Step 1: Start with One Stream & Expand

◈ Focus on **earning more from your primary income** (job, business).

◈ Add **side hustles** that complement your skills.

◈ Gradually invest in **passive income sources**.

Step 2: Turn Active Income into Passive Income

◈ Automate income streams (**investments, digital products, rental properties**).

◈ Scale businesses by hiring teams or outsourcing.

◈ Use **dividends and real estate income** to replace job income.

Step 3: Diversify Across Multiple Income Types

◈ Have at least **3-5 different sources** of income to protect against risk.

◈ Combine **active and passive** income streams for balance.

Step 4: Reinvest & Grow

◈ Use earnings to **buy more assets** (stocks, real estate, businesses).

◈ Avoid unnecessary spending—**focus on wealth-building.**

◈ **Example:**

A person with **a job ($5,000/month), dividend stocks ($500/month), real estate income ($1,500/month), and an online business ($2,000/month)** has diversified income totaling **$9,000+/month**.

9.4 Managing Multiple Income Streams Effectively

Once you have multiple income streams, you need a system to **manage, track, and optimize them**.

1. Use Budgeting & Tracking Tools

◈ **Best Apps:**

◈ **Mint & Personal Capital** – Track all income streams in one place.

◈ **QuickBooks & Wave** – Manage business income and expenses.

◈ **Google Sheets** – Create a custom income-tracking spreadsheet.

2. Automate Savings & Investments

◈ **Set Up:**

◈ Automatic contributions to **retirement accounts**.

◈ Reinvest profits from businesses & side hustles.

◈ Use **robo-advisors (Betterment, Wealthfront)** for hands-off investing.

3. Protect Your Wealth with Insurance & Risk Management

◈ **Health & Life Insurance** – Safeguards personal finances.

◈ **Liability Insurance** – Essential for entrepreneurs & real estate owners.

◈ **Asset Protection Strategies** – Legal structures (LLCs, trusts) to shield wealth.

9.5 Conclusion: Build & Secure Your Financial Empire

Multiple income streams **are the key to financial security and independence**. The more diversified your income, the **less vulnerable you are to financial setbacks**.

Final Steps to Financial Freedom:

◈ Start with **one side hustle or passive income stream**.

◈ Diversify into **at least 3-5 income sources**.

◈ Automate investments and reinvest profits.

◈ Protect wealth through **insurance, financial planning, and smart risk management**.

◈ **What income stream will you add first?** Let's start building your financial future today!

Chapter 10: Planning for the Future – Retirement and Financial Security

Financial freedom isn't just about making money—it's about **keeping it, growing it, and ensuring it lasts a lifetime**. Retirement planning and long-term financial security are crucial to enjoying life without financial stress.

Unfortunately, many people underestimate the importance of early retirement planning. They either assume Social Security will be enough or believe they can start saving later. **The truth? The earlier you start, the easier it is to secure your future.**

In this chapter, we will cover **how to build a secure retirement plan, maximize savings, and ensure lifelong financial stability** so you can enjoy a worry-free future.

10.1 Why Retirement Planning is Essential

Many people put off retirement planning because they think it's too early or they don't make enough money to start saving. The reality is:

◈ **Retirement is expensive** – The average retiree needs **$1 million to $2 million** to live comfortably.

◈ **You can't rely on Social Security alone** – It only replaces **40% of your pre-retirement income**.

◈ **The longer you wait, the harder it gets** – Compound interest works best when given time to grow.

◈ **Key Question:** How much money will you need to retire comfortably?

Factors That Determine Retirement Needs:

- **Expected lifestyle** (Travel? Downsizing? Healthcare needs?)
- **Inflation** (Prices will be higher in the future)
- **Healthcare costs** (Medical expenses rise significantly with age)
- **Lifespan** (People are living longer, requiring more savings)

◈ **Example:** If you need **$60,000 per year in retirement** and plan to retire for **25 years**, you'll need at least **$1.5 million saved**.

10.2 The Power of Compound Interest in Retirement Savings

Compound interest is the **most powerful tool** in retirement planning. The earlier you start, the **less you have to save each month** to reach your goal.

◈ **Example of Compound Growth:**

Starting Age	Monthly Savings	Total at Age 65 (7% Return)
25	$500	$1.2 million
35	$500	$600,000
45	$500	$300,000

◈ **Lesson:** Starting **10 years earlier can double your retirement savings!**

10.3 The Best Retirement Accounts & How to Use Them

To build wealth for retirement, you need to use **tax-advantaged retirement accounts**.

1. Employer-Sponsored Plans (401(k), 403(b))

◈ **401(k)** – Offered by private companies; employers often match contributions.

◈ **403(b)** – Similar to 401(k) but for teachers and nonprofit employees.

◈ **Why It's Important:**

- Contributions **reduce taxable income**.
- Employer matching is **free money**—always contribute enough to get the full match!
- Money grows **tax-deferred** (you don't pay taxes until withdrawal).

◈ **Example:** If your employer matches **50% of contributions up to 6% of your salary**, and you earn $50,000 per year, you get an **extra $1,500 per year for free!**

2. Individual Retirement Accounts (IRA & Roth IRA)

◈ **Traditional IRA** – Contributions **lower taxable income**, but withdrawals are taxed in retirement.

◈ **Roth IRA** – Contributions are **after-tax**, but withdrawals are **100% tax-free** in retirement.

◈ **How to Choose:**

- **If you expect to be in a lower tax bracket in retirement** → Use a **Traditional IRA**.
- **If you expect taxes to rise in the future** → Use a **Roth IRA** (better for younger investors).

◈ **Contribution Limits (2024):**

- **$6,500 per year** (or $7,500 if 50+).

3. SEP IRA & Solo 401(k) (For Self-Employed & Business Owners)

Self-employed individuals **can save more** for retirement with these accounts.

◈ **Contribution Limits:**

◈ **SEP IRA** – Up to **25% of earnings** (max $66,000 per year).

◈ **Solo 401(k)** – Up to **$66,000 per year** if self-employed.

◈ **Best for:** Entrepreneurs, freelancers, and small business owners who want **big tax savings** and **higher contribution limits**.

10.4 How to Calculate Your Retirement Number

To determine how much you need to retire, use the **4% Rule**.

◈ **The 4% Rule:**

- You can withdraw **4% of your retirement savings per year** without running out of money.
- If you need **$60,000 per year**, you need at least **$1.5 million saved** ($60,000 ÷ 0.04).

◈ **Steps to Find Your Retirement Number:**

1. Estimate **annual expenses in retirement**.
2. Multiply by **25** (to account for a 4% withdrawal rate).
3. Adjust for **inflation and healthcare costs**.

10.5 Creating Passive Income for Retirement

Relying only on savings isn't enough—you need **income-producing assets** in retirement.

Best Sources of Passive Retirement Income:

◈ **Dividend Stocks** – Companies that pay steady dividends (Coca-Cola, Johnson & Johnson).

◈ **Real Estate Rentals** – Rental properties provide monthly cash flow.

◈ **REITs (Real Estate Investment Trusts)** – Earn real estate income **without owning property**.

◈ **Annuities** – Insurance products that provide **guaranteed income** for life.

◈ **Goal:** Create multiple passive income streams so you don't have to **depend on just savings**.

10.6 Common Retirement Planning Mistakes to Avoid

◈ **Mistake #1: Starting Too Late**

◈ **Solution:** Start today—even small contributions make a difference.

◈ **Mistake #2: Not Taking Advantage of Employer Matching**

◈ **Solution:** Always contribute enough to get the **full 401(k) match**.

◈ **Mistake #3: Underestimating Healthcare Costs**

◈ **Solution:** Plan for **Medicare, out-of-pocket expenses, and long-term care insurance**.

◈ **Mistake #4: Not Diversifying Investments**

◈ **Solution:** Spread investments across **stocks, bonds, real estate, and income-generating assets**.

◈ **Mistake #5: Ignoring Inflation**

◈ **Solution:** Invest in assets that **outpace inflation** (stocks, real estate, etc.).

10.7 Estate Planning & Leaving a Financial Legacy

Retirement planning isn't just about **saving for yourself**—it's about protecting your wealth for your loved ones.

Key Estate Planning Strategies:

◈ **Create a Will & Trust** – Ensures your assets go where you want.

◈ **Assign Beneficiaries** – Make sure retirement accounts have updated beneficiaries.

◈ **Consider Life Insurance** – Provides financial security for your family.

◈ **Why It's Important:**

- Without a **will or trust**, the government decides how your assets are distributed.
- Proper estate planning **avoids legal battles and tax burdens for heirs**.

10.8 Conclusion: Take Control of Your Financial Future

Planning for retirement isn't about **hoping** you'll have enough—it's about **ensuring** it.

◈ Start investing **as early as possible** to maximize compound growth.

◈ Use **tax-advantaged retirement accounts** to build wealth efficiently.

◈ Create **multiple streams of income** to support long-term security.

◈ Avoid common mistakes and protect your wealth with **estate planning**.

◈ **Are you ready to take control of your financial future? Start today!** ◈

Appendix A: Tools and Resources for Financial Growth

Building financial security requires the right knowledge, tools, and resources. Whether you're budgeting, investing, building a business, or planning for retirement, the right tools can simplify and accelerate your journey. This appendix provides **a comprehensive list of financial tools, resources, and services** to help you manage money effectively, increase your income, and grow wealth.

A.1 Budgeting & Expense Tracking Tools

◈ **Why It's Important:**
Budgeting helps you **track income, control spending, and allocate money efficiently**. Without a budget, it's easy to overspend and struggle with saving.

1. Best Budgeting Apps

◈ **Mint** (Free) – Connects to bank accounts to track expenses and categorize spending.
◈ **You Need a Budget (YNAB)** (Paid) – Helps create and stick to a zero-based budget.
◈ **PocketGuard** (Free) – Tracks how much you have left after bills and savings.
◈ **GoodBudget** (Free/Paid) – Uses the **envelope system** to manage spending.

2. Best Spreadsheet Budgeting Templates

◈ **Google Sheets Free Budget Template** – Customizable and accessible anywhere.
◈ **Tiller Money (Paid)** – Automated financial tracking with Google Sheets integration.

◈ **Tip:** The best budget is the one you'll actually use! Choose a method that works for you.

A.2 Income & Side Hustle Platforms

◈ **Why It's Important:**

A **single source of income is risky**. These platforms help you start a **side hustle or freelance gig** to earn extra money.

1. Freelancing Platforms

◈ **Upwork** – High-paying freelance jobs in writing, programming, marketing, and more.

◈ **Fiverr** – Sell digital services like graphic design, SEO, and voiceovers.

◈ **Toptal** – For experienced freelancers (developers, designers, consultants).

◈ **PeoplePerHour** – Find small freelance jobs quickly.

2. Selling Digital Products

◈ **Etsy** – Sell digital downloads (planners, printables, art).

◈ **Gumroad** – Sell ebooks, courses, and software.

◈ **Teespring & Redbubble** – Sell print-on-demand (POD) products.

3. Dropshipping & E-commerce

◈ **Shopify** – Best for starting an online store.

◈ **Amazon FBA** – Sell products with Amazon handling fulfillment.

◈ **eBay & Facebook Marketplace** – Sell second-hand or bulk items.

◈ **Tip:** Choose **one** income stream and master it before adding another.

A.3 Investing & Wealth-Building Tools

◈ Why It's Important:

Investing is the key to **long-term wealth**. These tools make it easy to **invest wisely and grow your money**.

1. Best Stock Investment Platforms

◈ **Fidelity** – Best for long-term investors, no fees on most trades.
◈ **Vanguard** – Best for low-cost index funds and ETFs.
◈ **Charles Schwab** – Great for beginner investors.
◈ **M1 Finance** – Automates investing with **fractional shares**.
◈ **Robinhood** – Commission-free trading (but lacks retirement accounts).

2. Best Robo-Advisors (Automated Investing)

◈ **Betterment** – Manages investments with minimal fees.
◈ **Wealthfront** – Offers smart, automated investing and tax-loss harvesting.

3. Best Real Estate Investing Platforms

◈ **Fundrise** – Invest in real estate with as little as $10.
◈ **Roofstock** – Buy rental properties without managing them.
◈ **Arrived Homes** – Invest in fractional real estate properties.

◈ **Tip:** Start with **index funds (S&P 500 ETFs)** if you're new to investing.

A.4 Retirement Planning & Long-Term Wealth Tools

◈ **Why It's Important:**

Retirement planning ensures **financial security when you stop working**.

1. Best Retirement Planning Tools

◈ **Personal Capital (Free)** – Tracks net worth, investments, and retirement projections.

◈ **NewRetirement** – Helps calculate **retirement savings needs**.

2. Best Retirement Accounts

◈ **Fidelity & Vanguard** – Best for **IRAs, Roth IRAs, and 401(k) rollovers**.

◈ **Empower (formerly Personal Capital)** – Retirement investment management.

◈ **Tip:** Contribute to **401(k) employer matches first**, then **Roth IRA** for tax-free retirement.

A.5 Tax Planning & Business Finance Tools

◈ **Why It's Important:**

Managing taxes effectively **saves thousands per year** and ensures compliance.

1. Best Tax Filing Software

◈ **TurboTax** – User-friendly and great for beginners.

◈ **H&R Block** – Offers in-person and online tax filing.

◈ **FreeTaxUSA** – Free federal tax filing, cheap state filing.

2. Best Business Accounting & Tax Tools

◈ **QuickBooks** – Best for small business accounting.

◈ **Wave** (Free) – Good for freelancers managing invoices.

◈ **Bench** – Outsourced bookkeeping service.

◈ **Tip:** If you **make over $50,000/year in side income**, consider forming an **LLC or S-Corp** for tax advantages.

A.6 Credit & Debt Management Tools

◈ **Why It's Important:**

A strong credit score **saves money** on loans, credit cards, and mortgages.

1. Best Credit Score & Monitoring Apps

◈ **Credit Karma (Free)** – Monitors credit score and suggests ways to improve it.

◈ **Experian Boost** – Helps boost credit by reporting **utility & streaming bills**.

2. Best Debt Payoff Calculators

◈ **Undebt.it** – Helps create a **debt snowball** payoff plan.

◈ **ZilchWorks** – Calculates how fast you can be debt-free.

◈ **Tip:** Keep **credit utilization under 30%** to maintain a high score.

A.7 Learning Resources: Books, Podcasts, & Courses

◈ **Why It's Important:**

Ongoing learning helps you **stay ahead financially**.

1. Best Personal Finance Books

◈ **"The Millionaire Next Door" – Thomas J. Stanley** (Secrets of wealthy people).

◈ **"Rich Dad Poor Dad" – Robert Kiyosaki** (Mindset shift for building wealth).

◈ **"The Psychology of Money" – Morgan Housel** (Understanding money behavior).

◈ **"I Will Teach You to Be Rich" – Ramit Sethi** (Practical money management tips).

2. Best Finance Podcasts

◈ **The Dave Ramsey Show** – Debt payoff & financial discipline.

◈ **BiggerPockets** – Real estate investing.

◈ **ChooseFI** – Financial independence & early retirement strategies.

3. Best Online Financial Courses

◈ **Coursera – Personal Finance Specialization** (Free courses from top universities).

◈ **Udemy – Investing for Beginners** (Affordable investment courses).

◈ **Skillshare – Side Hustle & Passive Income Courses**.

◈ **Tip: Read one personal finance book per month** to stay financially sharp.

A.8 Final Thoughts: Using Tools to Build Wealth

The right tools **make managing money easier**, **increase income**, and **help you reach financial freedom faster**.

Best Next Steps:

◈ **Choose a budgeting tool** and start tracking your spending.
◈ **Pick one investment platform** and begin investing.
◈ **Start a side hustle** using one of the recommended platforms.
◈ **Use retirement planning tools** to estimate how much you need to retire.

Financial growth is a **lifelong journey**—but with the right tools and resources, **you can achieve wealth and security faster than you ever imagined**! ◈

◈ **Which tool will you start using today? Your financial future depends on it!**

Message from the Author:

I hope you enjoyed this book, I love astrology and knew there was not a book such as this out on the shelf. I love metaphysical items as well. Please check out my other books:

-Life of Government Benefits

-My life of Hell

-My life with Hydrocephalus

-Red Sky

-World Domination:Woman's rule

-World Domination:Woman's Rule 2: The War

-Life and Banishment of Apophis: book 1

-The Kidney Friendly Diet

-The Ultimate Hemp Cookbook

-Creating a Dispensary(legally)

-Cleanliness throughout life: the importance of showering from childhood to adulthood.

-Strong Roots: The Risks of Overcoddling children

-Hemp Horoscopes: Cosmic Insights and Earthly Healing

- Celestial Hemp Navigating the Zodiac: Through the Green Cosmos

-Astrological Hemp: Aligning The Stars with Earth's Ancient Herb

-The Astrological Guide to Hemp: Stars, Signs, and Sacred Leaves

-Green Growth: Innovative Marketing Strategies for your Hemp Products and Dispensary

-Cosmic Cannabis

-Astrological Munchies

-Henry The Hemp

-Zodiacal Roots: The Astrological Soul Of Hemp

- **Green Constellations: Intersection of Hemp and Zodiac**

-Hemp in The Houses: An astrological Adventure Through The Cannabis Galaxy

-Galactic Ganja Guide

Heavenly Hemp

Zodiac Leaves
Doctor Who Astrology
Cannastrology
Stellar Satvias and Cosmic Indicas
Celestial Cannabis: A Zodiac Journey
AstroHerbology: The Sky and The Soil: Volume 1
AstroHerbology:Celestial Cannabis:Volume 2
Cosmic Cannabis Cultivation
The Starry Guide to Herbal Harmony: Volume 1
The Starry Guide to Herbal Harmony: Cannabis Universe: Volume 2
Yugioh Astrology: Astrological Guide to Deck, Duels and more
Nightmare Mansion: Echoes of The Abyss
Nightmare Mansion 2: Legacy of Shadows
Nightmare Mansion 3: Shadows of the Forgotten
Nightmare Mansion 4: Echoes of the Damned
The Life and Banishment of Apophis: Book 2
Nightmare Mansion: Halls of Despair
Healing with Herb: Cannabis and Hydrocephalus
Planetary Pot: Aligning with Astrological Herbs: Volume 1
Fast Track to Freedom: 30 Days to Financial Independence Using AI, Assets, and Agile Hustles
Cosmic Hemp Pathways
How to Become Financially Free in 30 Days: 10,000 Paths to Prosperity
Zodiacal Herbage: Astrological Insights: Volume 1
Nightmare Mansion: Whispers in the Walls
The Daleks Invade Atlantis
Henry the hemp and Hydrocephalus

10X The Kidney Friendly Diet
Cannabis Universe: Adult coloring book
Hemp Astrology: The Healing Power of the Stars

Zodiacal Herbage: Astrological Insights: Cannabis Universe: Volume 2

Planetary Pot: Aligning with Astrological Herbs: Cannabis Universes: Volume 2

Doctor Who Meets the Replicators and SG-1: The Ultimate Battle for Survival

Nightmare Mansion: Curse of the Blood Moon

The Celestial Stoner: A Guide to the Zodiac

Cosmic Pleasures: Sex Toy Astrology for Every Sign

Hydrocephalus Astrology: Navigating the Stars and Healing Waters

Lapis and the Mischievous Chocolate Bar

Celestial Positions: Sexual Astrology for Every Sign

Apophis's Shadow Work Journal: **:** A Journey of Self-Discovery and Healing

Kinky Cosmos: Sexual Kink Astrology for Every Sign

Digital Cosmos: The Astrological Digimon Compendium

Stellar Seeds: The Cosmic Guide to Growing with Astrology

Apophis's Daily Gratitude Journal

Cat Astrology: Feline Mysteries of the Cosmos

The Cosmic Kama Sutra: An Astrological Guide to Sexual Positions

Unleash Your Potential: A Guided Journal Powered by AI Insights

Whispers of the Enchanted Grove

Cosmic Pleasures: An Astrological Guide to Sexual Kinks

369, 12 Manifestation Journal

Whisper of the nocturne journal(blank journal for writing or drawing)

The Boogey Book

Locked In Reflection: A Chastity Journey Through Locktober

Generating Wealth Quickly:How to Generate $100,000 in 24 Hours

Star Magic: Harness the Power of the Universe

The Flatulence Chronicles: A Fart Journal for Self-Discovery

The Doctor and The Death Moth

Seize the Day: A Personal Seizure Tracking Journal

The Ultimate Boogeyman Safari: A Journey into the Boogie World and Beyond

Whispers of Samhain: 1,000 Spells of Love, Luck, and Lunar Magic: Samhain Spell Book

Apophis's guides:Witch's Spellbook Crafting Guide for Halloween

Frost & Flame: The Enchanted Yule Grimoire of 1000 Winter Spells

The Ultimate Boogey Goo Guide & Spooky Activities for Halloween Fun

Harmony of the Scales: A Libra's Spellcraft for Balance and Beauty

The Enchanted Advent: 36 Days of Christmas Wonders

Nightmare Mansion: The Labyrinth of Screams

Harvest of Enchantment: 1,000 Spells of Gratitude, Love, and Fortune for Thanksgiving

The Boogey Chronicles: A Journal of Nightly Encounters and Shadowy Secrets

The 12 Days of Financial Freedom: A Step-by-Step Christmas Countdown to Transform Your Finances

Sigil of the Eternal Spiral Blank Journal

A Christmas Feast: Timeless Recipes for Every Meal

Holiday Stress-Free Solutions: A Survival Guide to Thriving During the Festive Season

Yu-Gi-Oh! Holiday Gifting Mastery: The Ultimate Guide for Fans and Newcomers Alike

Holiday Harmony: A Hydrocephalus Survival Guide for the Festive Season

Celestial Craft: The Witch's Almanac for 2025 – A Cosmic Guide to Manifestations, Moons, and Mystical Events

Doctor Who: The Toymaker's Winter Wonderland

Tulsa King Unveiled: A Thrilling Guide to Stallone's Mafia Masterpiece

Pendulum Craft: A Complete Guide to Crafting and Using Personalized Divination Tools

Nightmare Mansion: Santa's Eternal Eve

Starlight Noel: A Cosmic Journey through Christmas Mysteries

The Dark Architect: Unlocking the Blueprint of Existence

Surviving the Embrace: The Ultimate Guide to Encounters with The Hugging Molly

The Enchanted Codex: Secrets of the Craft for Witches, Wiccans, and Pagans

Harvest of Gratitude: A Complete Thanksgiving Guide

Yuletide Essentials: A Complete Guide to an Authentic and Magical Christmas

Celestial Smokes: A Cosmic Guide to Cigars and Astrology

Living in Balance: A Comprehensive Survival Guide to Thriving with Diabetes Insipidus

Cosmic Symbiosis: The Venom Zodiac Chronicles

The Cursed Paw of Ambition

Cosmic Symbiosis: The Astrological Venom Journal

Celestial Wonders Unfold: A Stargazer's Guide to the Cosmos (2024-2029)

The Ultimate Black Friday Prepper's Guide: Mastering Shopping Strategies and Savings

Cosmic Sales: The Astrological Guide to Black Friday Shopping

Legends of the Corn Mother and Other Harvest Myths

Whispers of the Harvest: The Corn Mother's Journal

The Evergreen Spellbook

The Doctor Meets the Boogeyman

The White Witch of Rose Hall's SpellBook

The Gingerbread Golem's Shadow: A Study in Sweet Darkness

The Gingerbread Golem Codex: An Academic Exploration of Sweet Myths

The Gingerbread Golem Grimoire: Sweet Magicks and Spells for the Festive Witch

The Curse of the Gingerbread Golem

10-minute Christmas Crafts for kids

Christmas Crisis Solutions: The Ultimate Last-Minute Survival Guide

Gingerbread Golem Recipes: Holiday Treats with a Magical Twist

The Infinite Key: Unlocking Mystical Secrets of the Ages

Enchanted Yule: A Wiccan and Pagan Guide to a Magical and Memorable Season

Dinosaurs of Power: Unlocking Ancient Magick

Astro-Dinos: The Cosmic Guide to Prehistoric Wisdom

Gallifrey's Yule Logs: A Festive Doctor Who Cookbook

The Dino Grimoire: Secrets of Prehistoric Magick

The Gift They Never Knew They Needed

The Gingerbread Golem's Culinary Alchemy: Enchanting Recipes for a Sweetly Dark Feast

A Time Lord Christmas: Holiday Adventures with the Doctor

Krampusproofing Your Home: Defensive Strategies for Yule

Silent Frights: A Collection of Christmas Creepypastas to Chill Your Bones

Santa Raptor's Jolly Carnage: A Dino-Claus Christmas Tale

Prehistoric Palettes: A Dino Wicca Coloring Journey

The Christmas Wishkeeper Chronicles

The Starlight Sleigh: A Holiday Journey

Elf Secrets: The True Magic of the North Pole

Candy Cane Conjurations

Cooking with Kids: Recipes Under 20 Minutes

Doctor Who: The TARDIS Confiscation

The Anxiety First Aid Kit: Quick Tools to Calm Your Mind

Frosty Whispers: A Winter's Tale

The Infinite Key: Unlocking the Secrets to Prosperity, Resilience, and Purpose

The Grasping Void: Why You'll Regret This Purchase

Astrology for Busy Bees: Star Signs Simplified

The Instant Focus Formula: Cut Through the Noise

The Secret Language of Colors: Unlocking the Emotional Codes

Sacred Fossil Chronicles: Blank Journal

The Christmas Cottage Miracle

Feeding Frenzy: Graboid-Inspired Recipes

Manifest in Minutes: The Quick Law of Attraction Guide

The Symbiote Chronicles: Doctor Who's Venomous Journey

Think Tiny, Grow Big: The Minimalist Mindset

The Energy Key: Unlocking Limitless Motivation

New Year, New Magic: Manifesting Your Best Year Yet

Unstoppable You: Mastering Confidence in Minutes

Infinite Energy: The Secret to Never Feeling Drained

Lightning Focus: Mastering the Art of Productivity in a Distracted World

Saturnalia Manifestation Magick: A Guide to Unlocking Abundance During the Solstice

Graboids and Garland: The Ultimate Tremors-Themed Christmas Guide

12 Nights of Holiday Magic

The Power of Pause: 60-Second Mindfulness Practices

The Quick Reset: How to Reclaim Your Life After Burnout

The Shadow Eater: A Tale of Despair and Survival

The Micro-Mastery Method: Transform Your Skills in Just Minutes a Day

Reclaiming Time: How to Live More by Doing Less

Chronovore: The Eternal Nexus

The Mind Reset: Unlocking Your Inner Peace in a Chaotic World
Confidence Code: Building Unshakable Self-Belief
Baby the Vampire Terrier
Baby the Vampire Terrier's Christmas Adventure
Celestial Streams: The Content Creator's Astrology Manual
The Wealth Whisperer: Unlocking Abundance with Everyday Actions
The Energy Equation: Maximize Your Output Without Burning Out
The Happiness Algorithm: Science-Backed Steps to Joyful Living
Stress-Free Success: Achieving Goals Without Anxiety
Mindful Wealth: The New Blueprint for Financial Freedom
The Festive Flavors of New Year: A Culinary Celebration
The Master's Gambit: Keys of Eternal Power
Shadowed Secrets: Groundhog Day Mysteries
Beneath the Burrow: Lessons from the Groundhog
Spring's Whispers: The Groundhog's Prediction
The Limitless Mindset: Unlock Your Untapped Potential
The Focus Funnel: How to Cut Through Chaos and Get Results
Bold Moves: Building Courage to Live on Your Terms
The Daily Shift: Simple Practices for Lasting Transformation
The Quarter-Life Reset: Thriving in Your 20s and 30s
The Art of Shadowplay: Building Your Own Personal Myth
The Eternal Loop: Finding Purpose in Repetition
Burrowing Wisdom: Life Lessons from the Groundhog
Shadow Work: A Groundhog Day Perspective
Love in Bloom: 5-Minute Romantic Gestures
The Shadowspell Codex: Secrets of Forbidden Magick
The Burnout Cure: Finding Balance in a Busy World
The Groundhog Prophecy: Unlocking Seasonal Secrets
Nog Tales: The Spirited History of Eggnog
Six More Weeks: Embracing Seasonal Transitions
The Lumivian Chronicles: Fragments of the Fifth Dimension

Money on Your Mind: A Beginner's Guide to Wealth
The Focus Fix: Breaking Through Distraction
January's Spirit Keepers: Mystical Protectors of the Cold
Creativity Unchained: Unlocking Your Wildest Ideas in 2025
Manifestation Mastery: 365 Days to Rewrite Your Reality
The Groundhog's Mirror: Reflecting on Change
The Weeping Angels' Christmas Curse
Burrowed in Time: A Groundhog Day Journey
Heartbeats: Poems to Share with Your Valentine
Dino Wicca: The Sacred Grimoire of Prehistoric Magick
Courage of the Pride: Finding Your Inner Roar
The Lion's Leap: Bold Moves for Big Results
Healthy Hustle: Achieving Without Overworking
Practical Manifesting: Turning Dreams into Reality in 2025
Jurassic Pharaohs: Unlocking the Magick of Ancient Egypt and Dino Wicca
The Happiness Equation: Small Changes for Big Joy
The Confidence Compass: Finding Your Inner Strength
Whispers in the Hollow: Tales of the Forgotten Beasts
Echoes from the Hollow: The Return of Forgotten Beasts
The Hollow Ascendant: The Rise of the Forgotten Beasts
The Relationship Reset: Building Better Connections
Mastering the Morning: How to Win the Day Before 8 AM
The Shadow's Dance: Groundhog Day Symbolism
Cupid's Kitchen: Quick Valentine's Day Recipes
Valentine's Day on a Budget: Love Without Breaking the Bank
Astrocraft: Aligning the Stars in the World of Minecraft
Forecasting Life: Groundhog Day Reflections

Bleeding Hearts: Twisted Tales of Valentine's Terror

Herbal Smoke Revolution: The Ultimate Guide to Nature's Cigarette Alternative

Winter's Wrath: The Complete Survival Blueprint for Extreme Freezes.

The Groundhog's Shadow: A Tale of Seasons
Burrowed Insights: Wisdom from the Groundhog
Sensual Strings: The Art of Erotic Bondage
Whispered Flames: Unlocking the Power of Fire Play
Forgotten Shadows: A Guide to Cryptids Lost to Time
Six Weeks of Secrets: Groundhog Day's Hidden Messages
Shadows and Cycles: Groundhog Day Reflections
The Art of Love Letters: Crafting the Perfect Message
Romantic Getaways at Home: Turning Your Space into Paradise
Purrfect Brews: A Cat Lover's Guide to Coffee and Companionship
The Groundhog's Wisdom: Timeless Lessons for Modern Life
The Shadow Oracle: Groundhog Day as a Predictor
Emerging from the Burrow: A Journey of Renewal
The Language of Love: Learning Your Partner's Love Style
Authorpreneur: The Ultimate Blueprint for Writing, Publishing, and Thriving as an Author
Weathering the Seasons: Groundhog Day Perspectives
Valentine's Day Magic: A Guide to Romantic Rituals
The Shadow Chronicles: Stories of Groundhog Day
Love and Laughter: Fun Games for Valentine's Day
AstroRealty: Unlocking the Stars for Property Success
The Groundhog's Path: A Guide to Seasonal Balance
Groundhog Day Diaries: Reflections in the Shadow
The Groundhog's Light: Illuminating the Path Ahead
Valentine's Traditions from Around the World
AI Wealth Revolution: Unlocking the Trillionaire Mindset
Love Rekindled: Reigniting Passion in Relationships
Single and Thriving: Self-Love on Valentine's Day
Emerald Legends: Mystical Tales of Ireland
Green Alchemy: Harnessing Nature's Magic
The Hearts of Horror: A Valentine's Day Nightmare

The Leprechaun's Guide to Wealth and Wisdom

Dancing with the Sidhe: Celebrating the Otherworld

Shamrocks and Shadows: Mysteries of the Green Isle

Emerald Energy: Harnessing Luck and Growth

The Gingerbread Golem's Valentine: A Sweetheart's Guide to Love and Enchantment

The Celtic Knot: Weaving Life and Destiny

Green Fire: Elemental Magic for St. Patrick's Day

Clover Chronicles: Finding Your Inner Luck

Ireland's Mystical Creatures: A Field Guide

Gingerbread Golem's Love Almanac

Prowl and Thrive: The Lion's Guide to Success

Love Alchemy: Transforming Your Life Through Heart Energy

WORLD DOMINATION: Woman's Rule 3:The New Life

The Midnight Rose: A Guide to Lunar Love Spells

The Forbidden Letters: Writing Your Own Love Prophecy

Luck and Lore: St. Patrick's Day for Modern Mystics

The Green Path: A Pagan Celebration of Renewal

The Dark Architect's Guide to Reprogramming Reality

Prankster's Paradise: A Guide to Harmless Hijinks

Manifest Your Reality: The Law of Attraction Simplified

The TARDIS Owner's Manual: Understanding the Doctor's Ship: *A complete guide to the TARDIS, its technology, secrets, and mysteries*

Starlit Romance: Astrology Secrets for Finding True Love

The Time Lord's Atlas: A Complete Guide to the Whoniverse: ***A breakdown of the locations, planets, and dimensions explored in Doctor Who***

Sweetheart Shadows: The Dark Side of Love and Attraction

February Fire: Reigniting Passion in Every Area of Life

The Self-Love Toolkit: 5 Ways to Embrace Who You Are

February Sparks: Ignite Your Dreams in 28 Days

March to Success: A 31-Day Action Blueprint
Ancient Paths: The 13 Sacred Principles of Dino Wicca
Echoes of Tomorrow: Navigating the AI Revolution
The Wellness Blueprint: Balancing Mind, Body, and Soul
Green Horizons: Sustainable Living for a Better Tomorrow
The AI Wealth Code: How to Make Millions with Automation
AI-Powered Creativity: Writing, Art, and Music for Profit
Extinction Rites: Rebirthing Your Soul Through Prehistoric Magick
Sacred Serpents tarot
Celestial Enchantment blank journal
Star Strains
Culinary Journeys: Exploring Global Flavors at Home
The Hollowvale Curse
The Hollowvale Harvest
The Egg of Transformation: Awakening Your Inner Power
Blooming Into Power: A Wiccan Guide to Spring Awakening
The Nightmare Nexus: The Third Doctor's Perilous Haunting
Digital Detox: Reclaiming Your Life in a Connected World
Ostara's Path: Walking the Spiral of Renewal
The Sacred Hare

If you want solar for your home go here: https://www.harborsolar.live/apophisenterprises/

Get Some Tarot cards: https://www.makeplayingcards.com/sell/apophis-occult-shop

Get some shirts: https://www.bonfire.com/store/apophis-shirt-emporium/

Instagrams:
@apophis_enterprises,
@apophisbookemporium,
@apophisscardshop
Twitter: @apophisenterpr1
Tiktok:@apophisenterprise
Youtube: @sg1fan23477, @FiresideRetreatKingdom
Hive: @sg1fan23477
CheeLee: @SG1fan23477

Podcast: Apophis Chat Zone: https://open.spotify.com/show/5zXbrCLEV2xzCp8ybrfHsk?si=fb4d4fdbdce44dec

Newsletter: https://apophiss-newsletter-27c897.beehiiv.com/

If you want to support me or see posts of other projects that I have come over to: **buymeacoffee.com/mpetchinskg**

I post there daily several times a day

Get your Dinowicca or Christmas themed digital products, especially Santa Raptor songs and other musics. Here: **https://sg1fan23477.gumroad.com**

Apophis Yuletide Digital has not only digital Christmas items, but it will have all things with Dinowicca as well as other Digital products.

www.ingramcontent.com/pod-product-compliance
Lightning Source LLC
LaVergne TN
LVHW022010200926
848481LV00007B/2325
9798348550639